BUILD CONFIDENCE & SELF-ESTEEM GUIDEBOOK

90 Awesome Techniques to Become Confident, Overcome Self-Doubt, Shyness and Improve Your Self-Esteem

A.V. Mendez

TABLE OF CONTENTS

The Daily Advantage

I tend to write books with lots of "mini-topics" in them. The reason is that I believe that success in any endeavor is the result of incremental improvements done and achieved daily and weekly. That's why most of my books are about small daily actions in everything that we do. It's not just about that one big thing. It's about 25, 40, or 70+ small ideas, that when combined, brings in the best result imaginable.

In addition, some of the things I write about aren't groundbreaking methods. They are mostly simple, easy-to-implement ideas that a lot of us already know about but choose not to implement.

My job is not to give you more information. If information is the key to success, then everyone with an internet connection will be more productive, self-confident, persuasive, emotionally healthy, physically fit, and financially rich already. We are in the golden age of information and we can get almost any info we need just from a simple Google search.

My job is to give you structure and to present the information in a way that will maximize your intention to act.

My job is to make everything as simple as possible for you so you don't quit from overwhelm.

My job is to show the importance of the ideas in this book so you'll have better incentives to do something about your problem.

This book will help you do all of that when it comes to your SELF ESTEEM AND SELF CONFIDENCE. Let's do this!

Introduction

I used to smile a lot. I am a generally happy person and I love making jokes. I don't remember the exact date but I remember when it all changed.

A friend of mine told me that I shouldn't open my mouth too much when I'm smiling because it shows the gap on my teeth.

Up until that moment, I never saw my tooth gap as something negative. I never saw it as something that would bother other people. It all changed when someone (who I'm not even super close with) pointed the gap on my teeth. After that incident, I started making fewer jokes. I became insecure whenever people look at me. My self-esteem went into an all-time low.

I lost my self-confidence and it took me 3 years to get it back again. I started working on myself. I created habits and implemented ideas that would bring my self-worth back again.

The ideas in this book are the same ideas that I used (and continue to use), not just in my personal life, but also in business and in my relationships.

I hope that this little book will bring value to your life.

It doesn't matter what your insecurities are. It doesn't matter where you are in life right now.

We all need confidence in ourselves for us to do great things.

What is Self-Confidence?

I define self-confidence as the general ability to believe in ourselves, that we can overcome any trials and problems that we may face in our journey.

In this book, I will give you 90 ideas that you can do to build your self-confidence. The goal is not to implement all the ideas - that's hard to do. The goal is to choose the ones that speak to you, and hopefully, you'll follow the action guide included in each chapter.

8 SECTIONS OF BUILD CONFIDENCE AND SELF-ESTEEM GUIDEBOOK

The book is divided into 8 sections. Each section discusses ideas that may directly or indirectly add to your self-confidence. For example, in section 7 about Physical Fitness, I talked about washing your hands so you can avoid getting sick. But how does this actually relate directly to self-confidence? Well, it doesn't. But being physically healthy and never getting sick actually affects how we look at ourselves. In that way, it affects self-confidence indirectly.

Here are the 8 sections that we will focus on in this book.

Section 1 - Choose to Be Great

The easiest way to be self-confident is to actually have the skills that you need on your chosen field. Self-confidence is easy when you're actually good at what you say you're good at. Self-confidence is easy when you believe in your greatness and your ability to get better.

Section 2 - The Power of Social Influence

Knowing how to connect with other people is an underrated aspect of self-confidence. When you know how to deal with people, self-confidence becomes natural. You become adept in talking and making conversations that leads to more money, better relationships, and higher self-esteem.

Section 3 - The Ability to Deal with Failure

Failure is inevitable, but having the ability to persevere in spite of failure is a skill you must master. This gives you the belief in yourself that you can overcome anything!

Section 4 - Strategies for Improving Self-Esteem

This section gives you simple strategies for improving your self-esteem. Things that you can do on a daily basis like Eliminating Mental Blocks and Killing Your Ego.

Section 5 - Things to Stop Doing

This section focuses on things that you should stop doing to gain more confidence.

Section 6 - Mental Toughness

When you're mentally tough, criticisms and problems do not affect you. This is what I lacked when I started my downfall from happy & jolly to reserved & insecure.

Section 7 - Physical Fitness

In this part, you'll learn why and how Physical Fitness affects your self-confidence.

Section 8 - Always Stay a Student

All the masters in their field always stay a student. They never stop learning. This gives them more advantage and a sense of confidence backed up by real skills and knowledge.

All of these sections, when combined, will lead to more self-esteem, more self-confidence, and less insecurities.

Now, let's get straight to the first section.

Section 1
- Choose to Be Great

Choosing to be great isn't a one-time decision. Choosing to be great means choosing to act every single day.

It's choosing to work on yourself even when you don't feel like it... It's about choosing to put in the work.... even when everybody around you says it won't work.

The first step to achieving maximum self-confidence is to put in the work every day no matter what.

Remember, it's easy to be confident when you actually have "the goods" as some people would call it. Focus on doing the work and self-confidence won't ever be a problem for you.

1 - Strive for Greatness Everyday

What does striving for greatness mean?

Does it mean that you have to be perfect every day? Does it mean that everything that you do should be considered "gold?"

Heck no!

Greatness isn't about that. Greatness is about the consistency of your action. It's about choosing to do the work every day, so you may achieve greatness in every aspect of your life in the future.

If you're a basketball player, it's about choosing to work on your game every day.

If you're a copywriter, it's about choosing to study the greats every day.

The key here is the word "every day."

Striving for greatness is a decision that you make every day. There's no shortcut besides the work itself.

Action Guide:

Ask yourself: Are you choosing to strive for greatness every day? Or do you only work hard on days when you are inspired and motivated?

Pros don't wait for motivation or inspiration, they just "do" – day in and day out.

2 - Practice Every day

It's not enough that you choose to strive for greatness every day, you also have to follow up on your decision.

So, you wake up and you said to yourself "I'm choosing to practice my copywriting skills today." Now, what is it that has to happen so you can get better?

Practice is the key.

What are the things you can work on today that will have a big impact in the future? What are the little aspects of your work that can affect your future results?

If you're a copywriter, you can practice writing headlines, writing bullets, writing introductions or creating offers.

If you're a basketball player, you can work on your dribbles, your footwork, your shooting or your layups.

Choose one small aspect of your field and work on it today. You don't have to practice everything about your work/sport/topic today. Start making small steps that can take you to where you want to go.

Also, expect that you won't master your field within months. Even Kobe Bryant, Tim Duncan, Michael Jordan, and LeBron James took years before they became a "complete" player. Even then, they still had their own flaws and imperfection. But the real fans don't really care, between them, they have a combined 19 championships after all.

Action Guide:

Find one aspect of your work/sport/skill/art that you can work on today.

Create a schedule about what you would work on for the week.

For example: For Week 1, you'll work on your Headlines. For Week 2, you'll work on your Product Benefits. Keep on practicing and keep on getting better every single week.

3 - Aim for Mastery

Mastery is a word that is hard to define because mastery is a moving target.

The 4-Minute Mile was considered the "mastery" of running in the early 1900s. But when Roger Bannister broke the record, the 4-minute mile became the norm.

Don't get me wrong, it's still hard to run a 4-minute mile, but it's not impossible anymore. It's not considered for Masters only.

So, mastery depends on how you define it. This year, you might define mastery in your industry (say you're an entrepreneur) as someone who sells 10,000 a year of whatever you are selling. Then 3 years from now, that 10,000 may change to 30,000. It's always moving, always changing.

Aim for what your field's currently mastery looks like and then adjust your aim as your industry evolves.

Keep on working and keep on watching how your field defines the word "mastery." If you don't, you'll wake up one day feeling like a Panda Bear in the middle of the city - nothing to eat but concrete walls.

Action Guide:

Define what mastery means in your field.

What are the things you should do so you can achieve mastery?

What will happen if you stop working and aiming for mastery? (Most likely, you become extinct and you get left behind by others).

4 - Be So Good They Can't Ignore You

Manu Ginobili was drafted on the 2nd round as pick #57 in the NBA's 1999 draft.

Nobody really knows him outside of the Spurs scouting team. Plus, at that time, foreign players aren't as highly regarded as they are today. By all stereotypes and expectations, Manu was just another player - someone you and I may never even see on an NBA court.

But Manu got better, from 1999-2002, he continued to develop as a player and he won MVPs and championships in the Euroleague. When he started playing in the NBA in 2003, he was a monster. Nobody expected him to be that good. He was so good that there's no way other coaches, players, and staff can ignore him anymore. They have to change strategies because of Manu Ginobili - and even back then, most teams have no answer for him.

Manu retired in August of 2018 with 4 championships. Not bad for a 57th pick.

I want you to have the same story as Manu. I want you to be so good they can't ignore you anymore. That doesn't mean you should be good starting from day 1. Just like everybody else, you work for it, you improve each step of the way. So, by the time the spotlight shines on you, you'll know exactly what to do.

Acton Guide:

It's not that hard to be confident when you're actually good at what you're doing. Before you achieve greatness, you have to aim for being good first. Being good means, you're regarded as one the future of your industry. Being good means having a reputation for being a hard worker. Choose to be good today, then aim for greatness afterward.

5 - Know Your Value

Most lowly individuals do not have a confidence problem. They have an insecurity problem.

They don't trust themselves enough that they will make the right decisions. They have some physical insecurity - it's either they're too fat, too thin, too short, or too tall. They never run out of excuses why they keep on failing. They don't believe in what they can do. They don't believe in their own worth.

This is obviously not a good thing. How do you expect other people to look at you as if you're valuable if you yourself don't see it that way?

As Jordan Peterson's said, "treat yourself as someone responsible for helping." You have to realize your own value before other people can.

Action Guide:

Know what you can bring to the table. Are you a good negotiator? Are you a good passer? Are you a good songwriter? Are you a good teacher?

Whatever your skills are, nurture them and show them to the world. We all have something to contribute to this world. It doesn't matter what it is. For some it'll be solving the water crisis, for some, it'll be as simple as being a mango farmer. One doesn't have to be "bigger" than the other. We're all unique with our own set of gifts. Our job is to use that gift in the best way possible.

Know your value before anyone else does.

6 - Know Your Topic

If you're a coach, a teacher, a CEO, a speaker, or a manager, then you have to know more about your topic than the majority of your market/staff/students/listeners.

It's easy to be more self-confident when you know that you've been preparing for "this" for a while now. It's easier to gain self-confidence when you know that all your preparations are now leading you to the promised land.

Vincent Van Gogh wasn't considered a genius until his death. Now his paintings are worth millions of dollars and are the most valuable pieces of art in the world. The good news for us is, you don't have to wait till you die before you get recognized. If you're good and you know what you're talking about, people tend to listen.

With all the platforms that we have nowadays, knowing your topic well means you'll be able to instantly share what you got, thus helping you reach more people and increasing your chances of success. It all starts with knowing what you're talking about. If you're a fraud, people will notice. It doesn't matter what your confidence level is at the moment. Be real, be authentic and know absolutely what you're talking about.

Action Guide:

Look at your field and find materials that you can study. If you're a football player, then watch the replays of the best football games. If you're a writer, then go read some of the best books out there. If you're a politician, go look at great leaders to copy or take inspiration from.

As someone who aims for mastery, knowing more things about your topic means unstoppable confidence that you can take on the world no matter what. Why? Because you came prepared for the battle. And that's all you could ever ask of yourself.

7 - The Power of Small Goals

Knowing your goals means knowing what to strive for.

The more goals you achieved, the more confident you get. Achieving your goals bring positive feedback, which then turns into more actions, then more confidence and so on… It's a loop. You set goals, you take action, you achieve your goals, you get positive emotions, then you take more action… and the cycle repeats itself.

Confidence comes from achieving mini-goals that you set every week. If your goal is to make a million dollars and you're only making $50k per year now, then it might take you years to achieve it and gain that positive feedback.

What you can do instead is set mini-goals. These are process related goals that are easier to achieve on a weekly basis.

For example, your goal this week is to earn an extra $500. That's more achievable than the $1,000,000 especially if you're salary is currently at $50k per year.

Focus on achieving that small goal this week. Sure, you should look at the long-term goal, but the more you think about the long-term stuff without taking action on the short-term, means you won't get any positive feedback. Thus, you are more likely to quit early and lose your self-confidence overall.

Action Guide:

First, know what exactly is your long-term goal. Be specific and define what it would look like achieving that goal. Second, list all the things that you need to do and achieve to meet that long-term goal. Remember, big goals consist of small goals. Winning the championship means you have to be on the playoffs first. Then you need to win the first round, second round, conference finals and then the finals itself. Take it one step at a time.

8 - Lay the Groundwork

Before you start constructing a building, the first step is always to start laying the foundation so it won't topple when disasters happen. Before you can start putting the cement, you need to have a steel foundation first that will serve as the backbone of the project.

It's the same in any field or skill. There are important basics that needs to be met before you become great at what you do.

The fundamentals may seem boring but it's exactly what you need to achieve mastery in your field. In fact, the fundamentals are the first thing that you should master. This gives you the initial confidence and the long-lasting confidence that you need in your journey.

Imagine a soccer player who doesn't know how to kick the ball - that would be dumb as heck. Imagine a basketball player who doesn't know how to dribble. Imagine a scriptwriter who doesn't know how to write dialogues. Imagine a guitar player who doesn't know the G-chord. Not knowing the basics means you'll suck at what you do.

Action Guide:

Know the fundamentals in your field. The basics may be boring, but it's also the main foundation where your confidence will come from. First things first, make sure that you work on it before you move on to the "advance stuff."

9 - The 1% Principle

This principle states that you should improve 1% every day or every week. Let's say that you are a starting comedian. If Bill Burr is considered a 10, then you're probably just at the 1 or 2 level. That means you still have a lot of work to do before you can play in the big leagues.

So how do you get to that level? How do you improve quickly?

The answer is the 1% Principle. Your goal every week should be to improve your jokes. Improve your timing, delivery and the jokes you write.

That means aiming for weekly improvements. If you improve 1% every week for 1 whole year, you'll be 48% better than you currently are a year from now. What does a 48% improvement mean to your career? That probably means more people laughing, more gigs, less awkward moments on stage or a possible gig with your favorite comedian.

Improving 1% every week is a confidence builder based on actually getting better. It's not just in your mind - you're not just being confident for no reason at all. You're being more confident because you're improving. You're starting to feel more and more confident each week that passes by because you are making progress. It's not fake confidence, it's something backed up by action and results.

Action Guide:

What are the things that you can do this week to improve by 1%? The good thing about 1% is it's doable. It's a small step, but when achieved consistently, becomes a snowball of success.

Make a list of things you can do this week to improve in your craft, art, business, job, or relationships.

10 - Have a Vision for Your Future

People who have a great vision of themselves for the future are usually the ones who make a difference.

When you know what you want to become, and when you're doing something about it, your confidence level rises up. And when your confidence level rises up, you tend to do more things that will have a positive effect on your end-goal.

A vision is something big for yourself. It's something hard to achieve and may take years to do so. But it's also something to look forward to. It's something that you think about before you sleep at night. It's something that you keep playing on your head until you fall asleep.

Action Guide:

Write down what your vision would look like.

Is it 5 championship trophies in your room? What would it feel like having them? How would the celebration playout? Define your vision and imagine how it would feel like achieving those things in the present moment.

Your vision does not have to be "to change the world."

Focus on what you really want. If your vision is 1 big house in California and a Ferrari, then, by all means, write it down or grab yourself a picture of a house and a Ferrari and look at it.

If your vision is a movie screening with 500 people for a script you've written, then imagine how that would look like. You have to conceive it in your mind before you can make it into reality.

11 - The Seinfeld Calendar Chain Method

Brad Isaac, a young comedian at that time asked the Legendary Jerry Seinfeld for advice on how to be a better comedian. What Jerry Seinfeld said has now become the stuff of the legends. It's so powerful that I personally know dozens of people who use this method in their field.

Seinfeld said that if you want to become a successful comedian, then you have to write new jokes every day. He said that Brad should get a calendar and put an X-mark every time he writes something new every day. The secret is in not breaking the chain. That means writing jokes every day and putting an x-mark on the current date when you finished writing a joke. The longer the chain is, the better.

The chain gives you positive feedback and gives you more confidence to keep going. Now, the chain doesn't make things easier. But it does motivate and inspire you to keep on going.

Longer chains = More confidence in your ability

More confidence in your ability = More positive feedback

More positive feedback = More actions

It's a loop. And it's a never-ending one.

Action Guide:

Go get yourself a physical calendar.

What task does someone in your field needs to do every single day to improve? What are the things you need to complete so you can become a "complete package" as the others would say.

Write an x-mark on the date on your calendar every time you complete the task. Put the calendar on a place you can easily see.

Keep writing, keep practicing, keep going to the gym, keep studying, keep learning. Keep the chain going!

Section 2 - The Power of Social Influence

Being able to talk and connect with other people doesn't seem like something that would really affect your self-confidence. But it does.

Knowing how to talk to other people leads to more confidence. If you look at it carefully, your goals and aspirations will require you to connect with others.

You need to learn how to connect with teammates, coaches, officemates, business partners, and customers.

Your ability to be social will play a big part in whether you'll increase your confidence or not. Just look at some introverted persons you know. You quickly assume that they're not confident. You quickly assume that they're shy and reserved. Other people think that way too. And when someone thinks that way about you, you already get stereotyped and judged based on your social skills.

It's a circle. The better you are at being social, the more people look at you in high regard, and the more confident other people become in your skills and abilities. Thus, giving you more self-confidence knowing that other people believe in you as well.

12 - Practice Small Talk

Most people think that small talk is a waste of time. That it's useless and doesn't serve any purpose at all. The truth is small talk is the gateway to great conversations.

Imagine seeing a girl on a bar, would you come up to her and immediately propose a marriage? No, because that would be ridiculous. First, you have to open up a conversation. Ask how boring the night is or how awesome is she finding that bar to be. Then you introduce yourself… and so on…

Some of the things you can talk about as an opener are:

-The weather
-His or Her job
-Entertainment: movies, songs, art
-Food
-Travel

The secret to being good at small talks is to ask the right questions. Questions that can't be answered by a yes or a no. Questions that will make them think a little.

Example:

1 - Would you rather have summer or winter? Why?

2 – What's your major in school? Why did you choose it?

3 – What's your job? What's the best thing about it?

You don't have to go deep in any of your "small talk" questions. Just ask something that would make them talk.

Let's say that you asked about her dream job, and she said she wants to be a dancer, talk about how awesome that is and encourage her to pursue it. Ask about her favorite dance routine or ask about anything related to dancing.

Action Guide:

Don't be afraid to start with small talk. It's the normal way to start a conversation and nobody is expecting you to come up with deep and philosophical topics unless you're in a setting that requires you to do so.

13 - Mirroring

Mirroring is mimicking whatever your conversation partner is doing.

We tend to like people who act and look the same as us.

Mirroring is about sending non-verbal signals that unconsciously say "hey, I'm just like you."

However, mirroring can be disastrous if you just completely copy what the other person does.

Mirroring is not just about doing whatever the person is doing. It's more of being in sync with what they are thinking at the moment. It's about being able to understand what they are talking about. If you just copy everything they do, they will notice it and the conversation will turn sour.

So how do you apply mirroring without looking creepy?

First, you focus on their words and the context of the conversation and not their body language. If you focus solely on the body language, you will find the conversation to be awkward, and you will stop paying attention to what he or she is saying.

Second, do not copy everything they do. I would say 60% of their body language is the safe zone. If they scratch their head, then wait for 2 seconds and scratch your eyebrow. It's not exactly mirroring but it's close. If they smile, then smile as well… you get the point.

Third, do not copy them immediately. Respond to their questions or ask something or mention something before you copy their actions. This will give you that gap before you copy what they did.

This also makes the conversation look natural. Imagine if you just do whatever they do immediately. That would look awkward and creepy.

Action Guide:

Follow the 3-step process of the mirroring method. Remember, you don't have to copy every single thing that they do.

Keep it natural.

Remember my example. If they scratch their head, then scratch your eyebrow. If they hold their mouth, then give it 15 seconds before you hold your mouth as well. Mix it up a little bit and make sure that you're still listening to whatever they were saying.

14 - Stop Fidgeting

Fidgeting is a sign of a troubled mind.

If you fidget during conversations, you're basically saying any of the following:

-I'm bored
-I'm uncomfortable
-I'm nervous
-I'm insecure
-I'm not confident about myself
-I don't find this conversation stimulating

Is this the message that you want to send your conversation partner?

Do you want to make her feel uncomfortable? Do you want to send the message that you're insecure and bored? Of course not. So be aware of what you do whenever you are having a conversation.

If you're uncomfortable, excuse yourself and get a hold of the situation in the comfort room. Fidgeting makes the other person uncomfortable as well and it has the potential to destroy your conversation.

Action Guide:

Always be aware of your non-verbal cues, especially the negative ones like fidgeting.

If you're nervous about the conversation, just be honest and tell the other person that you found the topic to be more than you can handle. I also found washing my face in the comfort room to be an

31

effective way to "wake myself up" and be back in the moment, so I can focus on the conversation and not my own feelings.

15 - Eye Contact

People who don't look at other people in the eye during conversation are usually the ones hiding something.

They may be ashamed of something they've done. Or they could be guilty, so they can't look that specific person in the eye.

Not looking the other person in the eye also shows that you are insecure, shy and unconfident.

When you're having a one on one conversation, it is recommended that you look the person in the eye at least 50% of the time. Some people get uncomfortable with too much eye contact. They feel like they're being judged. So, 50% is the safe zone in terms of eye contact.

If you're in a group conversation, look in the eye of the person who is talking. If you're the one who's saying something, look at different people after every point that you want to make. (That's around 3-4 sentences, then you look at the other person).

Action Guide:

Your eye contact is the gateway to understanding the other person. As corny as this sounds, you can actually see it in their eye if they are bored, happy, passionate or excited. You have to practice understanding what the other person feels just by looking in their eye.

Look in the eye of the person you're talking to 50% of the time.

16 - Posture

Your posture is another non-verbal cue that either says:

"I'm a leader, I'm confident and I'm powerful"

Or

"I'm weak, and I'm not someone to be taken seriously"

The famous Psychologist, Jordan Peterson talks about standing up straight with your shoulders back as Rule #1 is his book 12 Rules for Life.

He says that by doing this, we are producing the chemical serotonin that makes us feel great, awesome and powerful.

Having the right posture makes us feel good. Having the right posture immediately signals dominance, power, and confidence.

Whenever you feel down, I recommend that you follow Jordan's advice. Stand up straight with your shoulders back. This will immediately make you feel a little better. You see, whenever we feel defeated, we tend to hunch and just roll into our beds.

But winners do everything they can to get themselves back in the game. Your posture is not just a sign of dominance, it's also a message to yourself that you are the one in control. And I think that is powerful as you can get.

Action Guide:

Whether you're alone, standing or sitting. Always stand up straight with your shoulders back.

If you're talking to someone, and you want to make them feel comfortable, stand up straight with your shoulders back.

If you're talking to someone, and you want them to listen to every single word you say...

Stand up straight with your shoulders back.

17 - Identify the Alpha

If you want to be your best confident self, then you have to learn from the best. You have to find someone whom you want to imitate and learn from.

This is where Identifying the Alpha strategy comes in.

In every group, there will always be someone who acts as the unofficial leader. He says the right things; his posture is on-point and he have this charisma that everyone seems to be attracted to.

You can find these alphas not only in humans but even on animals like lions and wolves. Obviously, we can't go to the wild and check these alphas out. So, we have to stick to humans. The point though is ALPHAS are everywhere.

Okay, back to humans, we can find alphas at bars, sports events, a group of friends and other events with lots of male and female around.

The easiest example is going to a bar. Try to spot the alpha in the group and watch what he or she does all night long. The alpha is confident. The alpha doesn't need to talk all night long. The alpha attracts everyone around him or her.

Learn from their non-verbal cues more than anything. What they say is mostly irrelevant. Watch for their actions and their responses to different questions. You're obviously eavesdropping at this point, so try not to look at the group directly. If you can find a way to join the conversation, then that would even be better.

Action Guide:

You will find this suggestion ridiculous but I'm being serious here. Go get yourself a pen and a notebook before you go to a bar and go alpha hunting. Take note of the things they say and do. Try to understand why they act the way they act.

If you're brave, you can even ask the Alpha herself about the things she is doing and why she did them in the first place. Tell her that you're a researcher and you want to know more about human behavior.

Crazy suggestion?

Maybe.

But if you're serious about learning to become more confident and become the alpha in the future, then this exercise will be a valuable lesson for years to come.

18 - Have Sexual Confidence

We're sexual beings.

We all have sex drives that need to be met. It's something natural to us.

Being good in bed can bring a different type of confidence that may affect our performance at work or in our field of expertise.

Being good in bed means you're also making your partner happy. As they say, "happy wife, happy life" - and this also apply as "happy partner, happy life."

Aside from being more confident and happier, sex also gives benefits like:

-Lowers blood pressure
-Reduce the chances of prostate cancer
-Better immune system

Action Guide:

Study how to get better at sex. Hire a consultant or read books about being better in bed. The better you are at sex, the happier your partner becomes - this generally increases your self-confidence and self-esteem.

It's a win-win for everybody.

19 - The Art of Listening

Have you ever had a conversation with someone and it felt like they just "get it?" They understand you and it felt like you're the only person in the world.

The reason you felt that way is because the other person is listening to you. He's not interrupting, he's not trying to steal your thunder, and he's not letting the conversation go into other topics. His sole focus is to listen and make you feel good about yourself.

Listening is an art, and it's something everybody needs to learn. Listening is the gateway to understanding the other person. When you know how to listen, you automatically become confident about what you can and can't say to the other person. When you listen, you understand the other person on a deeper level.

The Art of Listening

1 - Listen with intent. What is the other person trying to say? What is she trying to convey? You can only learn this if you listen with intent.

2 - Do not think about some witty thing to say or some response that will steal the other person's thunder. Let them talk as much as they can. I found that if I talk for only 20% of the whole conversation, the other person tends to like me more and more.

3 - Avoid interrupting unless what you have to say can really add to the conversation.

4 - Smile and nod as a sign of approval.

Action Guide:

In your next conversation, apply these 4 tactics when listening to your conversation partner.

I guarantee you that your conversation will be better. I guarantee you that by the end of the conversation, your friend will like and trust you more.

Listening is about making the other person feel important. It's not about trying to say something smart or funny. It's about understanding what the other person feels at the moment.

When you know how to listen, you understand the other person better. And when you understand other people, you learn more about them which increases your social confidence fast!

20 - Make Friends with People Who Wants the Best for You

Friends can make or break you.

So, you have to choose the right friends. Friends who will be happy with your achievements. Friends who will not envy your progress in life.

Sure, envy is natural when it comes to friends. So, make friends who will use this envy as motivation to better themselves - instead of using that envy to hate you.

It's easier to be confident when you have a support system who wants the best for you. You feel more empowered, supported and loved.

How to Make Friends

Most of the time, we will have different paths with our friends. Some may be just starting out and we could be in the middle of the most important year of our lives. Some will stay at the job they hate while we will follow our hearts and start our dream business.

When this happens, we need to start making new friends. We're not really cutting our old friends in our lives, we're just adding new ones who are on the same path as us.

If you're an entrepreneur, then make other friends who are also starting their own businesses.

If you're a tennis player, then go hang out with other tennis players!

You will not only learn from them, but you'll also be able to connect with people who thinks and acts like you. This support system is crucial in having a better career (whether in sports, business, or corporate).

Action Guide:

1 - Find friends whom you can identify with.

2 - Find out where they hang out. If you're a copywriter, then you can meet other copywriters on marketing seminars or masterminds. If you're a basketball player, then the obvious hangout place is the basketball court. Wherever they are, go to those places and just start introducing yourself.

3 - Meet them on a weekly basis if possible. The more you hang out with them, the better you become in your field.

21 - The Power of a Smile

We like people who smile. That's an undeniable fact.

We even have the ability to know whether a smile is fake or not. Somehow, our brains are programmed to know the symmetry of a real and a fake smile. It's not 100% accurate but we know when it's real or not.

A smile gives us warmth and trust.

It gives us this feeling of being comfortable with the other person. When we smile, we become more confident because we feel at home.

"In the famous "yearbook study", they tracked the lives of women who had the best smiles in yearbook photos compared to the rest. Women who smiled the most lived happier lives, happier marriages and had fewer setbacks."

Action Guide:

1 - Smile in every opportunity you can. Smiling is a powerful agent that can stimulate a good conversation into a great one. This increases your confidence and other people's confidence in you as well.

2 - Learn the science behind why smiling is so powerful here:

https://buffer.com/resources/the-science-of-smiling-a-guide-to-humans-most-powerful-gesture

3 - If you don't smile a lot because of your teeth, then visit your dentist and ask what he can do about your situation. The money

you invest for a better smile is money well spent. Also, you don't have to have the perfect teeth to start smiling! Trust me, the warmth and the genuineness of your smile is much more important than having the perfect set of teeth.

22 - Practice Empathy

Empathy is about putting yourself in one's shoes as they say it. It's about understanding why someone would act a certain way.

What is he thinking? What problem he might be having?

What are the things in her mind that made her act that way?

When we know how to practice empathy, we become more open and we start to learn more. This makes us confident in our ability to connect with the other person.

Empathy is about understanding how someone feels. Empathy allows us to connect to a person on a deeper level. People like other people who seem to understand how they feel. When you have empathy, you don't say stupid things that may hurt others. You tend to say the right things that will make others feel better. Empathy is powerful, especially if you use it to make someone feel good about themselves.

Action Guide:

1 - Get more information before you start coming up with a plan of action or before you react to something. Knowing more about the other person or the situation means you'll be able to formulate a better response.

2 - Ask yourself, why did he act that way? What are they experiencing/feeling that triggered them to act a certain way?

Section 3 - The Ability to Deal with Failure

Our ability to deal with failure will dictate whether we will become successful or not.

Imagine being someone who understands what failure means. Imagine being someone who knows how to deal with failure. Imagine being someone so confident in his abilities that he sees failure as a setback and nothing else.

Failing is part of the game. All winners understand that. Even the best of the best in our fields do not succeed in every idea they implement.

When you have the ability to deal with failure, your self-confidence increases because you know that you can take on the world no matter what. It's a powerful skill to have and it's something that can take you to the next level.

23 - Acknowledge the Failure

The first step to turning a situation around is acknowledging the failure itself. It's impossible to move on to the next project or the next idea you have if you're still hang-up with the last one.

Whether it's in business, sports, relationship or any aspect of your job - failure is part of the process.

Did you lose a championship? Acknowledge it. Accept that it's going to hurt for a little while.

You failed a business you're working on for the last 2 years? Accept it. You did everything you can and the market decided that they don't want your product.

You didn't get promoted this year? Accept your fate and then plan for your next move. Sulk for a few days if you need to, but don't give up on the plan.

Action Guide:

Acknowledge and accept that not everything is going to be the way you planned it in your head. There are no guarantees in life. All you can do is:

1 - Do your best to get the results that you want.

2 - Trust the process.

3 - Take action on things you can control.

24 - Failure Porn

We are in the culture of "failure porn."

It has become cool to fail, because you now have something to post on Facebook or Instagram.

Let us be clear with the concept of negative consequential failure. If you are working 1 hour a day on a business and you quit after 1 month, then you failed because you're lazy. It's not because you're unlucky and not because your idea sucks. You fail because your actions didn't back up your ambitions.

This is the kind of failure that we see almost every day on Social Media. This is failure porn. We think that every failure increases our confidence - but the truth is, with failure porn, it only feeds our ego! Which is as dangerous as you can get.

Real failure is born out of the process. You create a product, you worked hard for it, you invested your hard-earned money and you market the product as best as you can - and then you still failed. This is the kind of failure that is valuable. This is the kind of failure that makes you grow.

It is failure born out of the process of actually doing sh*t. Not failure from your 1-month business idea.

Action Guide:

Are you action faking and treating your 1-month failures as if they're valuable? Or are you really doing your best in everything that you do, and learning from it every single day?

If you are action faking - then just stop what you're doing and embed yourself in the process of actually doing stuff.

25 - Learn & Apply the Lesson

You lost the championship. You failed your 3rd business idea and your heart broken. Your girlfriend broke up with you.

Everything hurts but you understand that you still have the ability to bounce back. Go cry yourself out for now...

Once you're done with the pain, now it's time to move forward.

Not it's time to plan for the new beginning. It's time to get ready for the upcoming season of your life.

What are the things that you did wrong on your last failure? What are the valuable lessons you can get from that experience? You have to go back to the failure and expect it to hurt, but the lessons you will get will always be etched in your mind. The more hurt you are because of that experience, the more you'll remember the lessons you'll get from that failure.

Action Guide:

Confidence comes from knowing that you learned well from your failure - and now, you're ready not to make the same mistakes.

Write the lessons you learned in a notebook. I personally have a notebook where I list all of my failures and the lessons I got from them.

For example, write a section called "Social Media Consultant Lessons." Then make a list of all the things you learned from running that business.

26 - Track Your Progress

Another important aspect of success is tracking your progress. The more you track your progress, the more confident you become about your idea or your chances of success. This is true especially if you are taking daily actions that are moving you closer to your goals.

The way you track your progress is through the results you are getting every week, every month and every year.

Now, you have to be realistic with your progress. You have to know your expected results that you'll get based on the time frame that you set for yourself.

Let's say that you're in the business of Social Media Management. Your main goal is to get your first client who will pay you $500 per month within 45 days. With this goal in mind, you know that progress means 2 things:

1 - Getting a client
2 - Getting paid $500 per month within 45 days

What happens if by day 11, you still got no client but you already talked to 9 people about your service - and they just happen to not take your offer? Does that mean you are having progress? Absolutely! You already talked to 9 people and you offered your services, they just didn't say yes. That means you are making progress and you're not just action faking! Track what you do in terms of client attraction and what you achieved on a weekly basis.

As long as you are making progress, and as long as you are getting closer to your goal - then you're giving yourself a higher probability of success in your field.

Action Guide:

Track your progress per week, month and year.

Your progress will depend on the goals you set for yourself.

If your goal is to write a 50,000-word novel in 90 days, then you should be writing at least 4,000 words per week.

Are you hitting that target? Make sure that you are because that's the first sign that you're moving towards your goal.

27 - Stay Calm

It's easy to freak out and panic when everything is going against your way.

A basketball season has its up and downs. You can lose 5 games in a row and come back roaring to win the next 10 games.

You may get 0 sales this week on your real estate business and then have 4 by the end of the month.

Your ability to stay calm is a valuable trait that everyone around you will notice and appreciate. The stress doesn't make you fold - heck, it only makes you stronger. That's the kind of person you want to become.

When your calm, people around you trust you more and they tend to have more confidence in you. They know that something is not right but they trust your abilities to get through it because of your unflappable and calm demeanor.

As kids would say nowadays, you're not "shookt!" You understand the situation and you're calmly planning for your next move.

Action Guide:

What are the current situations in your life right now that needs a calmer and unflappably cool type of head? What are the things that stresses you out on a daily basis?

Instead of freaking out about how nothing is going right, identify the sources of your stress and start finding solutions for your problems

28 - Probability Thinking

Knowing the probability of success gives you more confidence that what you are doing will work.

Enter Probability Thinking...

This method is about giving yourself the best chance of success by skewing the probability in your favor. Let's say that your kid wants to make $100 this summer by selling Lemonades. If he just put up a Lemonade store in front of your house, the probability of him making $100 will be based on how many people walk outside your house every day. Our job (or your job in this case) is to skew the probability on your kid's favor by having more people walk by your front lawn.

So you can do things like:

1 - Have a bigger sign so people will notice your kid's lemonade store.

2 - Offer another product so your kid has the probability to make more money.

3 - You can go door to door and help your kid sell the Lemonade.

By doing all these things, you are now giving your kid a higher probability of achieving his goal.

The more value skew you provide, the more confident you can be that you will achieve your goals... and the higher probability of success you will have.

Action Guide:

How can you increase the probability of success in your field?

Think of the things you can do to increase the chances of succeeding in your business.

Example:

Business: Social Media Consulting

What can you do to increase the chance of making money?

1 - Have someone on the phone to answer customer service
2 - Provide faster results
3 - Have a more professional website
4 - Add client testimonials to your sales page
5 - Add a bonus package on your service

These are just some of the things you can do to skew value in your favor.

If you know that you have a huge chance of success, confidence is easy to come by. Probability Thinking helps you have that.

29 - Prepare for None of It to Work

You can do all the things right and still come up short at the end of the day. You can implement your plan to perfection and something wrong may still derail your progress.

Such is the life of someone pursuing something great. It doesn't always end up the way you planned it on your head.

Prepare for none of it to work. That doesn't mean you're not expecting success. No. It only means that you understand that just because did the work, that doesn't mean that your success is guaranteed. Preparing for none of it to work means you have a Plan B. Preparing for none of it to work means you're ready and confident in your actions and your backup plans.

It sucks if it happens but it's better to be prepared than to be delusional and think that everything will go according to our plan.

Action Guide:

Your next business venture may not work. You may not meet your annual sales goal. You may not win the championship this year.

So, what? You're prepared for none of it to work...

What are you going to do about it?

Your best bet is to regroup and plan again.

30 - Reframe the Failure - "Good"

Your perception greatly affects how you see the world around you. If you think that rich people are evil, then you'll probably never be rich yourself. If you think that poor people are the only ones who will go to heaven, and your highest value in life is "going to heaven," then you will probably stay poor for the rest of your life. If those things are how you perceived things, then that is how you will react to the world around you.

When it comes to failure, it's easy to use it as a reason to say:

"I'm a failure so I'm stupid"
"I failed, that means I'm not good"
"I failed, that means I'm not worthy"

The best way to combat this is to reframe the failure. Former Navy Seal, Jocko Willink has a strategy for reframing all the bad things that happens to him.

"Good"

Failed your exam? Good. Now you can study more next time.

Failed your business? Good. Now you can look at what you did wrong and do better next time.

Stopped reading books? Good. Now you can focus on execution.

The point is not to be a fake optimist.

No.

It's about reframing something negative and using it as a reason to do something better.

It's about using "Good" so you can be Great.

Action Guide:

Make a list of things that didn't work out for you in the last few days or weeks. Once you got that list, write a re-frame of how you can look at those "failures."

Example:

"I didn't hit my goal of going to the gym 3x this week"

Good. Now go there 4x next week.

"I finished my novel but it sucks"

Good. Now you can spend more time re-writing your work.

"I wasn't able to get a meeting with the big-time executive"

Good. You can spend more time with your family.

True confidence comes from being a realist optimist. Start by reframing the situation and turn it into something positive.

31 - Dealing with Fear of Success

Even though they don't realize it, a lot of people around you don't take the leap because they fear what would they become.

'What if I succeed in this business and forget about my family?

"What if I win the championship this year, then everybody's going to expect me to win every year"

"What if I make $1,000,000 this year and all my relatives start asking for a loan?"

As crazy as these sounds, these are valid fears that many people have. It's called the fear of success. It's the fear of having a huge burden to bare (which usually comes with success).

Action Guide:

1 - Know what you really want. Do you really need a $1,000,000 per year business? Or is a $100k per year business better as long as you're only working 4 hours a day for it? You make the choice.

2 - Identify the fears that you have and talk to a therapist. Sometimes, we have commitment issues that need to be solved before we can move forward.

3 - Ask what the best- and worst-case scenario may look like if you actually achieved your lofty goals. If the best-case scenario far outweighs the worst, then you have your answer - keep going.

32 - Dealing with Fear of Failure

Another type of fear that destroys confidence and self-esteem is the fear of failure. This is the type of fear that destroys dreams and aspirations even before they started.

IF I FAIL THEN...

"No one's going to like me"
"My family will tell me 'I told you so'"
"Nobody's going to love me anymore"
"People will look at me funny"
"People will judge me for that one failure"
"People will laugh at me"

The problem with 99% of our excuses mask as fear of failure is that they are mostly about other people's opinion. But the truth is, other people's opinion doesn't really matter. The truth is, 5 years from now, no one is going to remember your failed business attempt.

They are going to judge you based on your wins. Even then, you shouldn't base your self-worth with your achievements.

Other people's opinion of you doesn't really affect you unless you let it.

Action Guide:

Make a list of the fears you have. Ask yourself if they are valid fears or if they're just fear of judgment from other people. Start mitigating the risk of failure by applying the probability thinking strategy from chapter 28. List your fears and start slaying them one by one. That's how you achieve real confidence. Knowing that you can take on the hardships that'll come gives you more character and more confidence that you can beat the odds no matter what.

33 - Spot New Opportunities

Most of the time, opportunities come from places where we didn't expect them to be. They also come at times when we least expect them.

Spotting opportunities is a skill that you need to master because opportunities come and go fast!

One moment, you have the chance of a lifetime, the next, you don't realize that you just let the opportunity pass you by.

Spotting opportunities is important because having this skill gives you the confidence to take calculated risks. Risks that are based on having a higher chance of success than failure. Risks that are worth taking.

Action Guide:

How to Spot an Opportunity

1 - Be open to change.

2 - Always be looking for it.

3 - Listen to other people's problems. A problem is just an opportunity in disguise.

4 - Take more action. The more things you do, the more opportunity comes up.

5 - Be open to taking calculated risks.

Section 4 - Strategies for Improving Self-Esteem

Self-Esteem, according to Eben Pagan can be two things:

One definition is, "A generalized feeling that you can cope with the challenges of life." This feeling comes as a result of cultivating abilities.

Another definition is, "Confidence in our ability to face the challenges of life and confidence in our right to be successful and happy about our success."

Self-Confidence and Self-Esteem work
hand in hand in how you view yourself as a person.
Do you see yourself in high regard?
Or do you see yourself as someone not valuable to society?

Building your self-esteem is crucial to self-improvement. That's why in this section, I will give you 20 strategies that you can do, to build a strong confidence foundation that you can rely on for years to come.

34 - Inevitability Thinking

This strategy is about setting yourself up for success by focusing on the conditions that will affect your action.

Let's say that your goal for this year is to become a better vlogger. To become one, you need to practice every day and record yourself for at least 5 minutes a day. However, this is not an easy task. By using inevitability thinking, you are going to set up conditions that will force you to record that 5-minute video. So, to force yourself to take action, you can do the following:

-Make a bet with your friend that you will give her $5 for every day that you miss recording a video.
-You can put all your equipment beside your bed, and when you wake up in the morning, you immediately record a quick video.
-Always charge your equipment daily and make sure that they are at 100% capacity.

By doing these things, you are making yourself more likely to take action and do your task. This gives you more confidence that you can achieve your weekly and monthly goals.

Action Guide:

1 - Identify the task that you need to do or the goal that you want to achieve.

2 - What can you do to make sure that you will force yourself to take action? The key here is to set yourself up for success - prepare the tools and set up the conditions you need for maximum success.

35 - Create a Morning Ritual

All successful people I know have a morning routine. It's something that you do to make you more productive and also make you feel good about yourself.

Call it a "me time" if you will...

It's something that you do for yourself. It's something that can help you set your day up for success.

Some people do yoga, exercise, drinking green juice or smoothies, go to the gym, pray, write, read, etc.

Now, I don't want you to go overboard here. Just follow a simple morning routine that makes you feel good about yourself - physically, mentally and emotionally speaking.

Action Guide:

Here's something that I recommend you follow (then improve on or change depending on what you prefer):

6:00 AM - Wake Up - Drink 1-2 Glasses of Water
6:05 - 6:15 AM - Do Some Stretching Exercise
6:15 - 6:30 - Read a Book or Write on Your Gratitude Journal
6:30-7:00 - Brush Your Teeth, Take a Shower, Listen to Audiobooks

That's it. 1 hour of self-care to help you set your day up for maximum confidence and productivity.

36 - Do Not Attach Your Net Worth with Your Self-Worth

It's unfortunate, but we live in a world where your value is predicated in how much money you make. People judge us with what house we live in, what car we drive and what clothes we wear.

But it doesn't have to be that way. Since you are in control of your perception, you can change how you look at yourself. You can change how you define your self-worth.

Remember this, your income does not equal your worthiness as a person.

You earning $50,000 more this year than the year before does not mean you've become a better person. You having a bigger house than all your friends don't mean you're more valuable as a human being.

Stop attaching your Net Worth with Your Self-Worth.

When you're gone, nobody will remember how much money you make. You will be remembered by how you treat people. You will be remembered as someone who cares about his employees. You will be remembered how much you care about your family.

There's something about being confident in yourself not because you're financially rich, but because you know that you're a good person. It's easier to sleep at night knowing that you're out here trying to make the world a better place - just by being a good example to others, just by being true to yourself.

Action Guide:

Are you attaching your "worthiness" with how much you earn? Do you keep comparing your income with your friends?

If so, then you will never be happy. The confidence that you get from "being richer" is fake and something people of quality doesn't care about.

Focus on being a good person instead.

Attach your self-worth with how good you are as a person, now that's a better comparison.

37 - Achieve Your Weight Goal (It's Not What You Think)

WOAH!

You wouldn't think I would say this right?

Should we be accepting and just love our body no matter what?

Well, yes.

But this isn't about the weight itself. My advice has more to do with being physically healthy. If you're underweight, then you have to look at your BMI and see what weight suits your height. It's the same thing if you are overweight.

Your body needs to be in its best condition for you to feel good about yourself, physically speaking.

It's hard to be confident about yourself when you hike with your friends and then 5 minutes into the hike, and you're done.

You have to take care of yourself. Confidence isn't just about mumbling words of affirmation. Confidence comes from having real results that you can see or feel.

Action Guide:

1 - Know the right weight that you must hit to become your best healthier self. Look at the BMI chart and set a weight goal for yourself.

2 - Create a plan of action that you will follow in to hit your weight goal.

38 - Step Out of Your Comfort Zone

Most of us never get out of our comfort zone. We just box ourselves in so nobody can hurt us. This is a problem, especially for those who have big dreams and aspiration. If you want to become an entrepreneur, then you're going to have to take risk - and quit your day job, that you hate anyway.

But most people lack the confidence to step out of their comfort zone. They just live in a bubble hoping that no one would pop it outside. If you're afraid of getting hurt, failing a business - failing anything - then you will never achieve anything that is great.

You getting out of your comfort zone is something that you have to do to achieve greatness. Stay there and you will also stay mediocre and miserable all your life.

Action Guide:

What are the goals that you have that require you to get out of your comfort zone? What are the things that you want to do but are afraid of because you might fail?

Here's something that could help you decide.

1 - Create a list of the worst- and best-case scenario for each goal.

2 - Ask yourself if the worst-case scenario trumps the best-case scenario.

3 - Rank the worst-case scenario from 1-10, 10 with 100% chance of happening.

4 - Rank the best-case scenario from 1-10, 10 with 100% chance of happening.

5 - Decide on whether to proceed or not.

39 - Eliminate Limiting Beliefs

We all have beliefs that need to get shattered or change if we are to achieve greatness.

For example, 10 years ago, I thought that earning more than $100,000 a year is impossible. As crazy as this sounds, I thought that white people are the only ones capable of doing it. I have this limiting belief that race has something to do with making more money. I keep listening to these guys on T.V. about how there's a wage gap between race.

This is a limiting belief that is just plain wrong in my opinion.

With the rise of the internet, everyone can now make as much money as he wants. Today, the market decides whether you're worthy of 6 or 7 figures or not. If you provide value in their life and you continue to solve their problems, 99.9% of the people wouldn't really care whether you're white, black or brown. IT JUST DOESN'T MATTER.

To achieve your goals, you're going to have to squash a lot of limiting beliefs along your journey. Some will be easier to squash and some will be harder. But the more you wake yourself up to the reality, the more successful you will become

Action Guide:

What are the limiting beliefs that you have that are affecting your confidence that you will succeed? Think about how you look at money, relationship, and business.

For example, do you think rich people are evil? If so, then how come that you want to be rich as well? These 2 beliefs just don't match.

If you believe that rich people are evil, then you will never be rich yourself because you will always associate being rich with being evil.

Replace your limiting belief with something better.

With our example, replace "being rich is evil" with "being rich is good because you get to help a lot of people."

Now, you have a better reason to go for your goal. You just squashed this limiting belief and changed it with something that will serve you and others for the better.

40 - Lessen Mental Blocks

I personally think that mental blocks come as we age.

But I remember when my mom used to say "The reason why you can't remember things is because you don't use your brain enough." It was a joke. But it's also true.

In my teens, I barely do anything that helped me improve the way I think.

Mental blocks happen when you suddenly can't remember what you're supposed to say or do. It's like it's in the tip of your tongue and you just can't find the right words to say it.

Mental blocks can affect the way we communicate, thus affecting our confidence to speak to others.

So how do we lessen mental blocks?

Simple, do mental exercises that use each part of the brain.

Action Guide:

Here are some exercises you can do -

1 - Review the multiplication table. Use flash cards and play with your kids so you can both learn at the same time.

2 - Draw a map of your town according to your memory. You can also look at Google Maps and then draw how you remember it.

3 - Write with your non-dominant hand. This forces you to use more brainpower and more will power. It's challenging enough that

your brain will be forced to use more power so you can write something that you wanted to write.

4 - Meditate for 10-15 minutes and calm your mind.

Check out this link to find more brain exercises that can help you sharpen your mind.

https://www.businessinsider.com/brain-exercises-that-make-you-smarter-2018-1

41 - Improve Your Public Speaking Skills

One of the things that will force you to improve your self-confidence is public speaking. They say that this is one of the top fears that most people have.

Public speaking can be scary, unpredictable and nerve-wracking. But it's also something that could take your confidence to the next level.

Imagine being someone who knows how to take control of the room. Imagine being someone that everyone listens to. Imagine being someone who knows how to bring laughter and tears at the same time.

It's hard, especially in the beginning, but the benefits of learning how to speak in front of people are endless.

Action Guide:

1 - Read books about Public Speaking. I recommend Ted Talks by Chris Anderson and any books from Dale Carnegie.

2 - Join and Attend a Toastmaster group. The Toastmasters will force you out of your comfort zone and it will help you develop more creativity through their programs and events. Check one out near where you live.

http://www.toastmasters.org/Find-a-Club

42 - Change Your Faulty Perception About Yourself

I don't know what is up with our generation but it feels like we are a generation of insecure people.

We don't take compliments well and we don't trust our own ability to do something good.

This is a dangerous kind of thinking because how can we expect to help others when we don't even trust our own selves?

One of the ways you can fight this insecurity is by making a list of things you love about yourself. You can also add your skills or the things that you can do on the list.

Action Guide:

1 - Make a list of all the things you like about yourself. Don't feel awkward about it, no one is going to read your list except you.

2 - Make a separate list of the skills that you know how to do. It doesn't matter how little or big that skill is. It could be as simple as washing your own clothes.

The point of this exercise is to show you that you are worthy because you have all these skills and accomplishments - and nothing can take them away from you.

43 - Hang Out with Friends Who Makes You Feel Better About Yourself

If all your friends are negative nellies, then it's time to move on and make new ones. You should have friends who want the best for each other. You should have friends who trust you and believe in your dreams. If all they talk about is gossip, and your values are not matching theirs - then it's time for a change. It's time to make friends who make you feel better about yourself. Now, that doesn't mean that you should make fake friends who always say what you wanted to hear.

No.

You make friends with honest people. You make friends with people who have the same interest as you. You make friends with people who hold the same value as you do.

Do this one thing and your life will be completely different a year from now.

Action Guide:

1 - Assess what friends you have right now. Should you be spending more time or less time with them?

2 - Make friends who have the same interest as you. If you want to become a songwriter, then hang out with other songwriters. If you want to become a successful entrepreneur, then hang out with other successful entrepreneurs.

3 - Find these potential new friends on their "hangout place." Each group has its own unofficial and official hangout place, and most of these locations are obvious. You will find entrepreneurs in NBI

meetings. You will find songwriters on songwriting boot camps. You will find tennis players on the court.

4 - Introduce yourself and find out more things about them.

44 - Develop Self-Care Activities

When you care about yourself, people tend to notice your glow. People are more attracted to you and they like to be around you more. That's why developing self-care activities is crucial in increasing the level of confidence in yourself.

Also, when someone doesn't take care of herself - you actually notice it - in how she speaks, how she dresses, and even in how her aura affects you.

When you take good care of yourself, you also attract the right type of people. You attract people who also want to do what you do. You attract people who also want to achieve something great.

It's a snowball effect and it keeps on rolling.

Action Guide:

Develop self-care activities that you can do daily or weekly.

Activities like:

1 - Have a weekly massage.

2 - Eat at an expensive restaurant every once in a while.

3 - Prepare a nice meal for your family.

4 - Have a "family day" and do family-oriented activities. The key here is to spend time with all your kids, your partner and even extended family members.

5 - Watch Classic movies. Movies that are proven to give audiences an emotional experience. I recommend The Godfather and Shawshank Redemption as a start.

45 - Remind Yourself of How Good You Are

Sometimes, all we need is a reminder of our own greatness. The poem by Marianne Williamson said, "it is our light, not our darkness that frightens us."

Are you always acting insecure and beaten? Do you always see the beauty in others but not in yourself? Do you always admire other people, but has never said a single praise in your own abilities?

Then it has to change. This is not about bragging. This is not about what you will do. This is about what you CAN do.

There's nothing wrong about recognizing your own talents. By recognizing yourself, you are giving yourself permission to do great things.

Every once in a while, it's nice to remind ourselves of our own greatness – and there's nothing wrong with that!

Action Guide:

Catch yourself whenever you're acting insecure and beaten. Be aware of your own emotions and be wary of how these emotions affect your life.

Doubting yourself and being insecure about your own shortcomings is normal behavior, but you cannot let these feelings get in the way of recognizing what you can do.

46 - Kill Your Ego

People always mistook the ego as self-confidence.

No.

Ego is dangerous. Ego doesn't have a place in our hearts. Ego is the voice telling you that you're better than everybody. Ego is the voice that says nobody can ever beat you.

Self-confidence is the belief in one's ability backed by a track record. If you're as good as LeBron James in basketball, then there's absolutely nothing wrong with saying you can beat anybody. But if you're a benchwarmer and you keep telling yourself that you're the "best in the world," then there's something wrong with you. Self-confidence is based on your real capacity. It's based on how hard you are willing to work to get better. Ego is just a voice saying you're the best - even though deep down, you know that you aren't.

Action Guide:

1 - Always know the difference between ego and self-confidence.

2 - When you notice yourself experiencing feelings of ego, tap your face softly and ask yourself this question: "Am I really confident about this or is this just my ego talking?"

3 - Read "Ego is the Enemy" by Ryan Holiday. It's a simple yet very powerful book about eliminating destructive ego in our lives.

47 - Stop Comparing Yourself to Others

Although there are some benefits of comparing yourself to others, the cons far outweigh the pros.

Comparing yourself to others is dumb and stupid.

Everybody has a different journey. We all have different set of circumstances. We all have different set of goals. We all have our own advantages and disadvantages. And no matter how you look at it, there will always be people who will have it better than you.

Comparing yourself to others is a confidence killer. In fact, it's one of the biggest, stupidest things that ever happened to modern humans - keeping up with the Joneses. It will never be enough; you will never be enough - that's the message that will morally kill us all.

Action Guide:

1 - Use envy as a fire starter. If you're envious because your friend got promoted and you didn't, then accept that you feel that way and use that experience as a motivation to get better. The funny thing is, once you've used that envy as motivation - that envy almost always seems to go away!

2 - Understand that comparing yourself to other people is stupid, especially if you're comparing yourself to someone with a completely different journey.

3 - Compare yourself to who you are yesterday instead of to who others are today. (I got the advice from Jordan Peterson).

48 - Let Go of Perfectionism

Are you one of those people who always want everything to be perfect? Look, I don't know anything about you but it is a possibility that your perfectionism is affecting other parts of your life - or it may also be affecting your progress in your field.

Why? Because perfection doesn't exist. There will always be something to improve. There will always be something to change.

But that's the reason why innovation and iteration exist!

Imagine if Apple waited before the iPhone is "perfect" before they launched it? Imagine if Apple never launched the iPhone! What world will we be living in?

The problem with perfection is perfection always moves. In 2007, the first iPhone was considered "almost perfect" at that time. In today's standard, that first iPhone is considered antique already.

Action Guide:

Perfection moves. So, don't strive for perfection. Strive for movement. Strive for progress instead.

As long as you are improving your products, skills or services - then you are moving towards perfection. Perfection that you will never attain. But that's alright, the most important part is you keep moving forward. That's all you can do, and that's okay.

49 - Stop Giving a Damn About Everything

Our minds are constantly bombarded by different messages.

We have T.V., Social media, newspapers, radio, etc.

We have commercials, movies, news, etc.

There's just so much information out there that we can't even focus on one thing anymore.

How are you supposed to be confident on your main expertise if you're constantly being distracted by all these things I mentioned above?

My advice is simple. Stop giving a damn about everything. There will always be something to watch, something to listen to, something to debate about... But the truth is, most of these things aren't going to make your life better.

They will just bring you stress, and probably more insecurity if you keep comparing yourself to what you see on t.v. or the internet.

Action Guide:

1 - It's okay to give no f*cks about stuff that most people talk about. Focus on improving yourself and focus on serving your purpose instead.

50 - Don't Forget to Reward Yourself

Whenever I hit my weekly goal, I always make sure that I reward myself with something. It could be a night out on a nice restaurant or a simple ice cream that I really wanted to eat all week long.

When we don't reward ourselves, what we do seems to never be good enough. We closed a big deal and we don't feel anything. It's just another deal. While this may be a good idea, it will eventually catch up on you.

You'll feel burned out and tired. You won't appreciate your successes anymore. It will dilute your achievements as if they were nothing to you. You obviously don't want this to happen.

Go on and reward yourself for a job well done.

Now, don't overdo it. Your achievement should match your reward. Got a promotion? Cool. Go treat yourself on a 3-day relaxation retreat. Do not buy the German car that is 10x more expensive than your last car.

Action Guide:

1 - Don't be too hard on yourself. Remember that there's nothing wrong with a little celebration.

2- Make a habit of rewarding yourself. This increases your belief in your own ability and capacity to do great work.

3 - Match your achievement with the right reward.

51 - Take Responsibility for Your Own Life's Choices and Results

In Jocko Willink's book, Extreme Ownership, he talks about being responsible for everything that happens in your life.

Yes, other factors will always have an effect on your own results. Some piece of shit drunk guy punches you. It hurts, and it sucks.

Now, what are you going to do about it? You can mope and cry all day long. Or you can get yourself a self-defense teacher, so the next time something like that happens, you are now prepared to defend yourself. That's extreme ownership.

Other people think that it is victim blaming. No, not at all. It's about taking responsibility for what you can control. It's about being a leader among boys. It's about "the man" - and this applies whether you're a man or a woman.

Stop blaming other people for your own misfortunes. Start taking responsibility for your own successes and failures. No one is going to feel sorry for you. Everybody is fighting their own battles and thinking about themselves. You might as well take extreme ownership of what you can control.

Action Guide:

1 - I highly recommend that you read the books "Extreme Ownership" and "The Obstacle is the Way"

2 - What are the things that you're not taking responsibility on? Stop being a damn victim and start being a leader.

52 - Treat Yourself As If You're Someone Responsible for Helping

I know that I already mention Jordan Peterson in this book a million times??? But you have to forgive me for doing it again.

His book 12 Rules for Life and his lessons helped me a lot in navigating a tough stretch in my life. One of my favorite rules from his book is "Treat Yourself As If You're Someone Responsible for Helping."

This means caring about yourself. This means giving yourself the best chance to succeed in life. This means thinking of yourself as someone important - because you are!

When you treat yourself as someone responsible for helping, you basically say to your subconscious that you are someone who can do great things in life. This brings more energy, passion and love out of you into a world full of pessimism and hate. If you think one person can't change the world, then wait till you see what you can do. I believe that statement with all my heart.

Action Guide:

1 - What are the activities you can do to make yourself feel important? Apply the self-care strategies I mentioned in idea #44 (Self-Care Activities).

(Activities like: massage, sports, exercise, nature sightseeing, etc.)

Caring for yourself reinforces the belief that, yes, you are important. Yes, you are worth it. Yes, you believe in yourself.

53 - Let Go of Your Inner Critic

Each one of us has our own inner critic.

It's the voice that says "you're not good enough." It's the story we tell ourselves about how we will fail every idea that we'll try.

This is the inner critic.

In a way, this voice is good because it helps us in assessing what we should do with our problems.

But it's a big problem because more often than not, this voice turns into pessimism. This voice that started as a constructive criticism becomes something that stops us from taking action.

Your inner critic is good, but only if we let it give us criticism that we can use to do better.

Action Guide:

Just be wary of your inner critic. It can both be a positive and negative thing for us - we just have to know when it is giving us constructive or destructive criticism.

Section 5 - Things to Stop Doing

Most books about self-confidence focus only on what you can do
to increase your belief and self-esteem. In this part, we will focus
on things that you need to stop doing to regain massive confidence
in your life.

These are things that we don't notice,
yet we already do ourselves.

These are things that decrease your self-esteem.
These are the actions that are making us a pessimist.

These are actions that don't serve any
positive purpose in our quest to self-confidence.

Stop doing these things and you'll immediately feel
a positive effect on your self-esteem and belief in yourself.

54 - Stop Blaming Other People

One of the most destructive habits you can have is the habit of blaming others. This habit reinforces the belief that you are "never at fault." And when you have this belief, you never take responsibility for anything in your life.

Your car broke down… it's the dealer's fault.
Your girlfriend broke up with you… it's her fault.
You failed your exam… it's the teacher's fault.

This is a destructive habit that you need to stop doing, or else, you will live all your life thinking that other people are responsible for your failure.

Nothing can be further from the truth, that all the failures or success in your life is 100% entirely because of you.

You're the one who's making the decisions. You're the one who's taking (or not taking) action.

You could've checked and maintain your car every day but you didn't. You could've realized that your girlfriend is not happy with how you treat her. You could've studied more for your exam, but you didn't.

Stop blaming other people, because most often than not, you could've done something to avoid or eliminate the issue at hand.

Action Guide:

1 - Look back at the problems you had in the past couple of months.

2 - Think of the things that you could've done better to either avoid the problem or lessen its impact on you and other people.

3 - Forgive yourself for the mistakes you made in the past.

4 - Identify the lessons that you can learn from that experience. Ask yourself, what can you do better so the next time this problem comes up, you'll be prepared to implement a better set of solutions.

55 - Stop People Pleasing

Do you feel like you have to say yes to every request that other people have? Do you feel that you have to gain approval of all your family and friends?

If so, then you are a people pleaser.

Trying to gain approval from the people around you is a destructive habit and belief that will make you miserable. If you're always trying to get someone's approval, you're not really helping yourself become more confident and become more of an independent thinker who owns up to his or her own ideas.

Continue to do this and eventually, you'll start to attach your self-worth to whether X guy says your cute or Y stranger says you look like a rich person.

If that happens, then your self-esteem will always be dependent on other people.

Action Guide:

1 - When was the last time you try to please people because you want to gain their approval? Are they really that important in your life that you need to have their approval?

2 - Ask yourself, why are you spending so much time trying to please people you don't even like?

56 - Stop Idolizing Hollywood

Look, I understand the appeal.

We are hardwired to admire people who are famous. We are attracted to someone who has a high social status.

That's why we keep idolizing Hollywood celebrities as if they are perfect.

Most often, we even compare and copy what celebrities do.

Jennifer Lopez can dance, so we must dance too.

The Kardashians has big butts, so we must have big butts too.

Kylie Jenner is a billionaire at 22, then why aren't we? (and this makes you miserable because you keep comparing yourself to her).

Stop idolizing Hollywood celebrities. They aren't perfect, far from it. Hollywood has one of the highest divorce rates in any group of people in the world. Most of them don't really care about you, then why would you spend so much time trying to be like them?

Focus on yourself. Focus on your own abilities. Focus on what you can do to make the world a better place, one small action at a time.

Action Guide:

Do you find yourself copying other celebrities? Then stop doing it!

Whose celebrity are you trying to copy these days?

Look, we're all guilty here. I once bought a jacket that Ryan Gosling wore in one of his movies because I like to be as cool as him. Obviously, that didn't work out.

Stop trying to please people cause honestly, most people just do not give a flying f*ck about you.

57 - Stop the Constant Negative Thoughts

We're all prone to this trap.

We think of one negative thought and suddenly, tens of negative thoughts just come rushing through us.

One moment, you could be thinking about watching Netflix and then a few minutes later, you start thinking about….

…the laundry that you need to finish (neutral thought)
…then you start thinking about getting fired from your job if you do not wear the prescribed attire
…then you worry about being in debt
…then you worry about divorce because your wife cannot take it anymore
… and many more negative thoughts

This is not only a confidence killer but also an anxiety builder!

You need to be aware of your own thoughts so you can stop it before it gets worse. If you don't, then you'll get sucked in the vortex and you'll fill yourself up with anxiety.

Action Guide:

1 - Be aware of your own feelings. Notice immediately when you start having these negative thoughts.

2 - Replace the negative thoughts with what you can do instead. Focus on the solution that you need to do or the tasks ahead of you.

3 - Calm your mind by practicing a few minutes of meditation.

58 - Stop Putting Other People Down

Most people think that success is a zero-sum game. That you have to tear other people's building before you can build your own. This destructive mindset will stop you from ever building something worth admiring.

You don't need to bring people down just so you can rise up. It doesn't matter what your industry is. Sure, competition is always going to be there - and you need to do everything you can to survive. But do it morally. Do it the right way.

Instead of saying bad things about your competition, focus on building your product's reputation instead. Provide so much value to your customers that they have no choice but to switch to your product or service.

Focus on how you can improve your skills, expertise, product, or services instead of focusing on what others can and can't do.

This is a mindset based on good value and character. And it's something that will serve you for the rest of your life.

Action Guide:

Are there any aspects of your life where you're trying to constantly bring people down? In your relationships? In your work? Be honest with yourself here and tell the truth! If you are currently practicing this destructive belief, don't worry because there's still hope. You can still change this belief.
Focus on building yourself and other people instead. Honestly, it's just so much better to live that way.

59 - Stop Envy

I used to be envious with the success of my friends.

So and so gets promoted... Some dude earns 2x more money than me... X person finally bought his dream car at age 25...

I was happy for my friends but then this feeling of envy starts creeping in.
I felt like a failure.

Then I started finding a solution on my issues and I found a way to turn envy into motivation.

Here are the simple steps I do every time envy creeps in.

Action Guide:

1 - I accept the feeling. I accept and acknowledge that I am being envious.

2 - I ask myself. Do I really need to be envious? Am I willing to do what they do so I can get the same things? I'll start imagining what it feels like to be them, what I have to do every day to get the things that they have.... Most of the time, the sacrifices that they (I) have to do isn't just worth it. So I'll just go back to my reality and be me instead.

3 - At this point, the envy is dying. Now, use this time to muster motivation and inspiration from it. If your friends can do it, then you can do it too! Except this time, you'll do it your way!

60 - Stop Dramatizing

Negative things always happen.

We'll get rejected by a distributor. We'll get rejected by a client. A customer won't pay his balance. Some thug will steal your inventory.

These things suck! But do they really suck that bad that you have to act like a drama queen and have a fit? Is it the end of the world? Is your business not going to continue to survive? Is getting rejected by 1 client means the end of your business?

Don't get me wrong, these things are unfortunate and you should find a solution for them. But there's no need to over dramatized things. No need to act super emotional about it. There's no need to unreasonably blame everyone around you.

Here's what you can do instead...

Action Guide:

Assess the situation. Is it really that bad? No? Good. Yes? Then find a solution to the problem instead of being a drama queen about it.

Next, take note of what happened and come up with a solution so it won't repeat itself in the future.

61 - Stop Living in the Past

We all have our own successes in the past that we like to look back on. We all have our own "glory days."

There's nothing wrong with looking back. But if you start living more in the past than the present, then that's when the problem begins.

When you live in the past, you're never mentally present with your conversations. You always bring up the times when you did this awesome thing and another awesome thing...and so on...

But this clearly isn't good. You need to be in the present. The present where you can still do things, achieve more stuff and create better experiences. Focus on the present, because it's the only real thing that we have.

Action Guide:

It's okay to relieve the glory of the past. It's okay to be reminiscent of the good times. But remember that all we have is the present. There's a reason why the famous quote said that the "present is a gift." Because it's the only thing that is ever guaranteed. The past is gone and the future is only the consequence of our current actions. Focus on the present and be grateful for what you have right now.

62 - Stop Being Ungrateful

Ungrateful people are the worst.

Heck, I used to be one. I always thought that I have it worse than everybody else.

And then I started changing my perspective.

I started noticing what I have instead of what I don't.

Everything got better for me when I changed my perspective.

You can sulk all day why you still don't have a million dollars or you can be grateful that you're earning $5,000 a month while the rest of the world is living on $1 per day.

Stop being ungrateful. It doesn't serve any purpose and it'll only make you hate the world.

I know that this sounds easier said than done. I know that each one of us has different experiences. Just know that it's possible to turn a negative event into a positive one - and it all starts with changing your perspective.

Action Guide:

Every day, write at least 2 things you are grateful for. Grateful people are proven to be happier and more successful. Choose gratitude. Choose to be a person of positivity.

63 - Stop Counting Your Failures

Are you focusing too much on your failures?

Do you always remember all the "epic fails" that you have?

Then you need to change that.

You know that focusing on failures is bad for you, let's go straight to what you can do instead.

Action Guide:

1 - Count your successes instead. This increases REAL confidence and validation.

2 - Practice the art of learning from your failures. If you're going to remember your failures anyway, you might as well get something from it.

3 - Remember that a failure doesn't have to be attached to your self-worth. Good people fail all the time. What matters most is what you do after that failure. Do you fight or do you back down? Your response to a failure is what separates the strong from the weak. Be strong, be brave – always!

Section 6
- Mental Toughness

When you're mentally tough, failures become temporary setbacks. When you're mentally tough, you know that you can get through any hardships no matter what.

It's not about being good at ignoring the problem or "faking it till you make it." Being mentally tough means having a mind built and ready to take on struggles, failures, and problems.

In this section, I'm going to give you practical ideas that you can apply to build a strong resistance to failures. I'm going to give you exercises that you can easily do so you can build mental toughness quickly.

When you're mentally tough, you get to build confidence matched by a real belief in what you can do.

64 - The Power Negative Visualization

Did you expect this advice? Probably not. We should always all be Mr. Positive, right? Not quite.

The Stoic (Greek Philosophers) have this ancient practice of negative visualization where they think about the possible hardships and negative things that may happen to them. After doing the exercise, they will contemplate on the possible consequences of these negative things. They will ask themselves, is it really that bad? Does failing on this thing will make me miserable?

The truth is, most of our worst-case scenario isn't really something to be afraid of. Lose your job? That sucks but you can always find another one! Failed a relationship? That sucks too, but you can now find a better partner for you!

Negative visualization isn't about being pessimistic. It's about using the power of perspective so you can face your fears.

Action Guide:

1 - I recommend that you practice negative visualization at least twice a month. Doing this makes you gain perspective, confidence, and gratitude for what you currently have.

2 – Read more about Stoicism through www.dailystoic.com (not my website).

65 - Let Positive Thoughts Come In

The reason why I recommend that you only do negative visualization twice a month is that I don't want you to get drowned out by the negativity. Negative visualization is great for getting perspective - but I don't believe that it's something that you should do every day.

I believe in being a positive person. I believe in seeing the good in people. I believe in letting positive thoughts more often than the negative ones.

Positive thoughts are thoughts of inspiration, motivation or any possible action that may serve others.

Positive thoughts aren't just about affirmations (although it's a big part of it). Positive thoughts are also about believing that you can achieve great results with the skills that you currently have (and currently developing).

Action Guide:

1 - Practice positivity by doing affirmations daily. Say things that make you feel good about yourself.

Example:

"I am a good person"
"I am a value creator"
"I care about other people"

2 - Be a positive realist. That means acknowledging when things aren't exactly the way you want them to be, but at the same time,

still having the positive mindset and unwavering belief that you can get through it.

66 - Remember Your Death

This is another one I got from the Stoics.

"Memento Mori" - roughly translates to "Remember Your Death."

This means acknowledging that you only have a limited time here on Earth. It means being aware that in any time, nature, the universe or God can take your life away from you.

When you contemplate on your mortality every once in a while, you tend to take more calculated risks. You start doing the things you know you should be doing.

When you contemplate on your death, you start to love more. You start to become more thankful for what you have. You become more confident in taking action and following your dreams - because the truth is - you have nothing to lose! You are going to die. That's the only guaranteed thing in our lives. Use your remaining time well because we don't have any idea whether we'll still be here tomorrow.

Action Guide:

1 - Practice contemplating on your death every once in a while. It's also good to practice this whenever you're making a big decision... When you are trying to decide on whether to follow your dreams or not.

2 - Ask yourself, "If I die tomorrow, would I be able to say that I lived a good life?" If not, then you know that it is time for a change.

67 - The Snowball Effect

A snowball gets bigger and bigger the more you roll it down the hill. When momentum is on its side, then it gets bigger super-fast!

It's the same with our confidence. The more things we achieve, the higher our confidence gets. So, what's the key to having a big snowball.

First, you start with a small snowball that you can hold in your hand. Then you add more snow… and more snow… and more snow… and then you start rolling it, more and more until you achieved the largest snowball you can create.

With our ideas, the key is to start something, no matter how small that is. That's the crucial part that I want to impart with you. You will never be able to create something big if you aren't willing to start small.

You can build a snowball of success but you have to actually do the work. You need to create momentum first before you can start rolling the ball.

Action Guide:

Do you have a set of actions planned but unfortunately never did anything about it? Do you still believe in your original goal enough to actually act and start a snowball?

If you do, then you must start rolling the ball now and not think about every barrier (problems) that you may encounter. Just do it as Nike's slogan says… then let it flow, let it flow, let it flow.

68 - Always Believe in Yourself

I know that this is cliché advice. Believe in yourself, always believe, blah blah blah...

But there's a reason why this advice has become a cliché. BECAUSE IT'S TRUE AND IT'S USEFUL.

Believing in yourself isn't about faking your way to success. It's about acknowledging the skills and knowledge that you currently possess. Believing in yourself means knowing what you are capable of.

Action Guide:

This advice is common sense (or common knowledge) and many people even gets put off by it (they say things like "believe in myself, OKAY" with the tone of sarcasm).

But the issue with most common-sense advice nowadays is COMMON SENSE DOESN'T ALWAYS MEAN COMMON PRACTICE.

So, are you actually practicing this advice? Or do you just shrugged it off and say "okay?"

Make sure that you value yourself enough to the point that you 100% believe in what you are capable of doing and achieving.

69 - Specific Based Words of Affirmation

I already mentioned this in the chapter about positivity. I recommend that you use this strategy if you are someone who has constant doubts about yourself.

If you are someone who's always negative about everything, then practicing words of affirmation can rewire how you think.

Words of affirmation are words that make you feel good about yourself. These are words that inspire and motivate you to do more. These are words that affirm what you are capable of.

The way you can maximize the power of affirmation is to use it specifically based on what you do for a living.

Action Guide:

Create words of affirmation based on your job or whatever your specific goal is. Let's say that you want to be the best Financial Advisor at your company. Then your words of affirmation may look like this:

"I am a great Financial advisor"
"I care about my clients"
"My priority is my clients"
"I am changing other people's lives for the better"
"My clients love me because I give the best financial advice"
"My clients love me because I always bring value to the table"

Specific based affirmation is a powerful tool in inspiring and motivating yourself, thus helping you increase your confidence in everything that you do.

70 - Be Persistent

Steve Jobs once said that he believes that the only thing that separates successful people from the ones who aren't is one's ability to persevere through hardships.

When you are persistent, you always stand back up. You keep trying new things and you keep taking calculated risks. When you are persistent, you keep on discovering new options and new opportunities for yourself.

I'm not exactly sure whether you can manufacture persistence or not. But I do feel that it's something hardwired in each one of us. It's something that we get based on our experiences. It's something that is generated by our own "whys" (the reason why we do what we do). So, if you want to be persistent, then you have to know your why - your reason for doing and being.

Action Guide:

Answer these questions.

Why do you do what you do? What do you want to get out of it? A car? A house? Time Freedom?

Next, ask yourself why you want what you want. Now we get a little meta. Asking why you want what you want helps you in knowing yourself more. Knowing why you want what you want is crucial in understanding what makes you tick as a person.

This is powerful stuff.

As Friedrich Nietzsche said, "He who has a why to live for can bear almost any how."

71 - Be Prepared

Imagine this, there are 2 singers who joined the X Factor (and both are 19 years old). The first one has been singing since she was 12 and been practicing her skills every day for the last 5 years. The second can also sing, drinks alcohol and eats ice cream every day - and she joined just because she wants the money.

Guess who will be the one more confident and ready? Guess who will be the one who has a higher chance of winning.

The one who prepared for that moment all her life or the one who joined X Factor so she can win a (1) million dollars?

The answer is obvious.

If I'm a betting man, then I will make my bet on the first one. Why? Because she's the one who prepared for it. She's the one who's been honing her skills every day for the last 5 years.

Action Guide:

1 - Be prepared to hone your skills in whatever you are trying to do and achieve.

2 - Create the habit of practicing and getting better at your chosen field. If you are a marketer, then study the best marketers in history. If you are a chess player, then record your games and study what you did right and what you did wrong. Always be improving - that's the mantra that you need to follow from here on.

72 - Practice Solving Problems

This is the secret to becoming a value creator. When your mindset is used to solving problems (yours or other people's), you tend to operate on a higher level than most people.

A problem solver focuses on the solution. He doesn't complain, or mope, or do nothing.

He simply finds the solution, plan and executes.

A problem solver is someone whom other people like to be around with. When you are a problem solver, you become a person of value. You become someone who has a higher social status - not because you are famous, but because you know how to help other people.

Action Guide:

How to Become a Problem Solver

1 - Learn to identify other people's problems. You can always find other people's concern through the words they are using.

Be on the lookout for words like:

This sucks
I hate this
I wish there was
How can I do X things
Is there any way to do X while not doing Y?

"I hate this job"

What can you do for this guy so he won't have to hate his job anymore?

"I wish there was a better way to travel to work"

What can you create to make this one a reality? (Uber was born because of this question)

Identify the trigger word and find the problem.

2 - Make a plan of action that you can execute to solve the problem. Find the best solution/s and help solve the problem for other people (or help solve it with them).

Section 7 - Physical Fitness

This will probably be the oddest section in this book. Why? Because physical fitness isn't particularly discussed by most people when it comes to confidence.

But what you probably don't know is that physical fitness and energy has a direct effect on how you perceive yourself. And how you perceive yourself affects your confidence.

I recommend that you keep an open mind and try out the simple ideas in this section. Trust me, you being in better shape will affect the way you see yourself.

You having more energy will give you the ability to do greater things.
You being more physically fit will help you achieve your mission and be at your best self.

Doing the ideas in this section may not instantly make you more confident, but on the long-term, they will prove beneficial to your success - and I'm 100% sure of that

73 - Sleep Like a Baby

Sleeping has always been a problem for me. I've always had a mind that's running 24/7. It feels like I never run out of things to think about. This may be good especially if you're a beginner in your field. You get things done and you're always on the go. But this will catch up to you - making it harder for you to get a regular sleeping schedule.

One thing I found out the hard way is resting is as important as working. I used to have an erratic sleeping schedule. Sometimes I would sleep at 3am and the next, at 9pm. This messed up my circadian rhythm and made me sleepy in the morning and wide awake at night. My ability to focus suffered and I became 50% less productive.

Every doctor will tell you this: You need at least 7 hours of deep sleep, it is crucial for getting our mind and body ready for the next day.

Action Guide:

Here are the things that you can do to help you have a good night sleep.

1 - Cover your whole room with blinds. The darker it is, the better.

2 - Use 5-HTP as a supplement in helping you sleep. (Consult your doctor first before you follow this advice)

3 - Stop using any electronic device 2 hours before you sleep.

4 - Stick to a regular sleeping schedule. This is the most important part of having a good night sleep.

74 - Drink Water Every Day

I know. You already heard this advice a million times. But there's a reason why you keep hearing it - because it's a piece of important advice.

You already heard it, but are you doing it?

Are you drinking 8 glasses of water a day just like the "common advice" says?

If you're like most people, then you're probably not drinking enough water. The best solution I found for this problem is to keep your water as close to you as possible.

Prepare your water and put it somewhere where you can grab it quickly.

Make It Fun and Tasty

One of the reasons why we don't drink as much water is because water tastes nothing. It's boring.

What you can do is make fruit infused water so you can make your water more refreshing. Prepare your infused water the night before and have at least 6-8 glasses full of servings.

Action Guide:

1 - Set yourself up for success. Put your water near your work desk and all over the house if you work at home.

2 - Watch some infuse water recipe on YouTube and start creating your own. This will make drinking water an event and not just some boring task that you need to do.

75 - Stretch, Stretch, Stretch

This is simple advice.

When you start feeling dizzy or tired or when you're already running out of energy - just stand up and start stretching.

Your body isn't made to sit all day. We are made to move. Also, sitting all day may cause back pain in the long term.

So, I highly recommend that you do stretching exercises every hour.

If you are following the Time-Chunking technique, then you can work for 50 minutes and then use your rest time as your stretching time. A 2-minute stretching exercise will help you immensely in gaining focus and will make you feel refresh for the next task.

Action Guide:

1 - Go search for 2-5-minute stretching exercises on YouTube. If you're working in an office and you have no place to do your stretching, then do desk exercises that don't require you to stand up.

Resource:

https://www.youtube.com/watch?v=Lg8PFfd85ts

76 - Meditate

One of the ways to increase your focus and peace of mind is by meditating. When I mention to people that I meditate, I always get a look of confusion or reluctance to say anything. I get it. Meditation for some, is still kind of woo-woo. Maybe not as much as before but it still is in some places.

Also, meditation has this stigma that you have to sit still for 1 hour a day and do nothing.

I'm still a beginner in meditation but I already felt the benefits of meditation even after just a few months of doing it. I'm more focus, calmer and even more confident because it's helping me get more things done. It also helps me think clearly about complicated things in my life.

Action Guide:

Here's how I do my meditation:

1 - I go to the corner of the room and sit still "Indian style."

2 - I set a timer for 20 minutes (You can start with 2 minutes if you've never had a meditation session before).

3 - I put my earplugs so I don't hear as much noise around.

4 - I close my eye and I breathe in and out for 3 seconds each.

5 - I focus on the sound of my breath. Having an earplug also makes me feel my breath a little bit more than usual.

6 - I stop when I hear the timer rings.

77 - Wash Your Hands = Never Get Sick Again

An average adult American gets sick/common cold at least 3-4 times a year. If you think about it, that's around 4-8 weeks of your year!

1 week of being sick + another week of recovery = 2 weeks of torment!

Whenever you get sick, you may start to feel better after 4-5 days but that doesn't mean that you're already at 100%. You still need another week to fully recover. If you get sick 4 times a year, that's 8 weeks of unproductive time that you could've used in getting shi* done!

This is another common advice that will help you eliminate or lessen the times you get sick per year.

Your hands touch everything; Your laptop, other people, your pens, your books, etc. And then it touches your mouth, ear, eyes, and nose. Aside from the air itself, this is where sickness begins.

You can eliminate a lot of your "potential sickness" just by washing your hands at least 4 times a day.

Action Guide:

1 - Buy an alcohol/hand sanitizer that you can use if you're not anywhere near a place where you can wash your hands.

2 - Wash your hands with soap at least 4 times a day.

This advice may not directly affect your confidence but it will affect every aspect of your life. It's just so much easier to be confident when you're healthy - and that's a fact.

78 - Take Care of Your Voice

I have never heard a self-help coach or author talk about this. Your voice is your main communication device. It is what you used to influence other people. It is what you use to connect. It is what you use to teach.

Without your voice, it's going to be so much harder to achieve high status and gain the confidence of other people. Without your voice, you will have a hard time communicating what you want to say.

If you're a speaker, a teacher, an online coach, a singer or anyone who uses her voice to make an impact - then this will be even more important to you.

Action Guide:

So how do we take care of our voice? How do we make sure that we're not abusing it? Here are the things you can do to protect it:

1 - Avoid screaming every day. This will damage your voice faster than anything.

2 - Drink less coffee and alcohol. Water is the best lubricant for your voice.

3 - Do some voice exercise at least 5 minutes per day. Search for "Roger Love" on YouTube and follow his advice. He's the real deal and he coaches Eminem and other famous people in various industries... The exercises look and sound dumb - but they work!

4 – Avoid speaking when you are sick.

79 - Maintain a Healthy Weight According to Your BMI

I almost didn't put this chapter in this book. Why? Because I know that there are some people who will get offended by it.

I want you to know that I'm not fat shaming or anything like that. All I want is to give you an idea that will help you in every aspect of your life - one of those is having your ideal weight based on your BMI.

Your BMI helps you in calculating the ideal weight for your height and gender. BMI doesn't take into account your race, ethnicity and body composition. However, it is widely accepted by doctors, nurses and other health professionals.

Action Guide:

Calculate your BMI according to your height and gender. This will give you a clearer idea of what your weight should be like. It's not 100% accurate but it's a reliable starting point.

Check out the following websites:

https://www.heartfoundation.org.au/your-heart/know-your-risks/healthy-weight/bmi-calculator

https://www.nhlbi.nih.gov/health/educational/lose_wt/BMI/bmicalc.htm

https://www.cdc.gov/healthyweight/assessing/bmi/index.html

80 - Take Care of Your Hearing

This is another uncommon one. You won't hear self-help coaches talk about your ears/hearing. But it's an important aspect of your physical health. Your ears are the literal gateway to communication and information.

We don't realize this but we all suffer from noise pollution. We just get used to the noise so most times, we don't even notice it. But that is dangerous because it can lead to hearing loss at an early age.

Always protect yourself and be aware of your environment.

Action Guide:

Here are some action steps you can follow to protect your hearing:

1 - Clean your ears with a cotton swab (Q-tip) at least twice a month. We don't need to go crazy with this. We just need proper maintenance to make sure that our ears are clean.

2 - Avoid places with mega loud noises if possible.

3 - Use earplugs when you're in a loud environment.

4 - Have a "noise free" vacation and go to a peaceful place - a beach or a farm is recommended.

Section 8
- Always Stay a Student

Someone who is truly confident is someone who should always stay humble. Look, life is hard - and no matter how confident you are, there will always be someone trying to replace you or your business.

Sure, you could be confident in your ability to be the best in the market. But once you stop learning, that's when competition swoops in and take your place.

My advice is simple...and this is beyond being confident....

Always keep learning. Always stay a student.

If you have the mind of a student who constantly wants to learn, your competition will have a harder time trying to replace you. Constantly learning means you can be confident that you are always on the cutting edge in your field. It means you'll continue to improve more and more.

Confidence is easy if you never stop learning.

81 - Read Books Everyday

I love books. Books have always been the main catalyst in every life-changing decision that I made (and will make).

I love books because I can get someone's perspective on different topics for as low as $0.99 cents. I love books because I can learn new things fast without spending thousands of dollars, unlike online course, seminars or workshops.

Books are so valuable you can find pieces of yourself where you never thought you would.

If you want to be more confident, then you have to keep learning - and reading books is one of the best ways to do that.

Action Guide:

1 - Identify the topics that you want to understand more.

2 - Buy books in bulk so you can save money.

3 - Read books at least 60 minutes a day.

4 - Take written notes or use a highlighter to take note of the most important parts of the book.

5 - Read books that you find harder to read. This will force you to improve your comprehension.

82 - Take Online Courses

We're lucky that the price of learning online has gone down massively in the recent years. Today, we can get a $30 online course about our chosen topic and learn almost all the basics that we need to thrive in our market.

There used to be an online course apocalypse from 2007-2015 where gurus are charging $3,000 for the same information you can get for $50 online. I'm just glad that the hype died down and we are now pricing the online courses accordingly.

Today, you have no reason not to learn anything. Every information that we need is already there at our fingertips. You just have to commit to learning and improving.

Action Guide:

1 - Identify what topics you need to learn or improve on.

2 - Checkout platforms like Udemy, Masterclass, Teachable, Lynda, and Thinkific.

3 - Search for your topic and buy an online course with good reviews.

4 - Commit to finishing the course! Most people stop taking the course in the first module! Commit to learning and continue to get better every day.

5 - Take notes and ask, how can you use this information to help you achieve one of your goals?

83 - Attend Seminars, Workshops, and Bootcamps

Some skills require you to "be there" to maximize your learning. Let's say you want to become a professional basketball player. Then attending a boot camp about dribbling the ball will be much better than reading a book about basketball. Doing the actual thing is the action that is going to make you better. If you're a game developer, having someone walk you through the entire process in person is going to help you internalize the steps - which will make you a better game developer.

Networking

Another major aspect of seminars and boot camps is networking. With boot camps/seminars, you are going to meet a lot of like-minded people. People who are on the same path as you. I believe that this is where the value is in attending seminars and workshops. The lessons you'll learn are going to be useful but the people you meet in these events will be even more valuable. Use this opportunity to find a possible business partner, investors, mentors, accountability partner, and new business friends.

Action Guide:

1 - Commit to attending at least 2 seminars, workshops or boot camp every year.

2 - A good seminar shouldn't cost you more than $500 for a one-day event, and no more than $3,000 for a 3+ day event. Be careful about who you give your money to! Lots of $5,000++ workshops just aren't worth the price!

84 - Hire a Coach

A coach is someone who will watch over you. Someone who will criticize your mistakes and get you in the right track. Someone who can teach you the best ways to approach problems in your market. Someone who will serve as your accountability partner.

But a coach isn't someone who will guarantee your success. Never, ever rely on somebody else when it comes to your future. No one is going to be your messiah. No one is going to be your lifesaver. You have to do the work yourself. A coach can guide you through the way - but he can never do the work for you. A coach may give you the guidance - just like a GPS helping the driver get to his chosen location. But a coach can never drive you to your destination.

The best thing about hiring a coach is the feedback that you will constantly get in the process. This feedback is the most valuable part of coaching. The feedback means you can pivot and adjust your strategies as you move along the process. A good coach will always be giving you honest and truthful advice, remember to use it wisely.

Action Guide:

1 - Attend seminars and workshops to meet like-minded people.

2 - Focus on what you can offer the other person. If you want someone to coach you, you either have to pay or do some kind of work for him. You need to provide something of value - something that will make his time worth it in exchange for teaching and helping you.

3 - Ask for other people's feedback about the person. Does he have a good track record? Is he actually successful in the field that he's

teaching on? Or is he just a 22-year-old "life coach" who got his certification from a $20 online seminar?

85 - Start Teaching

One of the tricks to learning more about a topic is to start teaching it. The more you talk about something, the more you realize what you don't know.

Teaching what you know to other people will give you a new perspective about what you teach. There's something magical about learning new things while you teach a specific topic to others. Most of the time, these new breakthroughs will come from questions that your students/friends will ask. You will learn how to look at something in a new light. You'll discover perspectives that you've never had before.

You will also start to gain more confidence in what you do as you see more people learning from you.

The more you teach, the more you learn. Now, that's magic.

Action Guide:

1 - Identify what topics you are good at.

2 - Listen to your friends' problems. What is it are they complaining about? Can you help them solve the problem? Do you have enough knowledge or experience that you'll be able to give them a working solution? If yes, then you can start by teaching your friends how to solve that problem.

3 - Ask your Facebook friends, "who needs help with X?" Offer your expert advice for free at first. Find someone you can help and share your knowledge with as many people as possible.

86 - Find a Long-Term Mentor

Finding a mentor is hard. A mentor isn't someone you pay monthly as a retainer - that's a coach.

A mentor is a fatherly (motherly) figure who will guide you in your whole journey. A mentor is someone whom you consider one of the most valuable people in the world. A mentor is someone you would consider part of the family.

A mentor is someone who will give you tough love - which you'll then realize as something you need so you grow and get better.

Relationship

Long term mentors are found through relationships. It's almost impossible to find a mentor just by asking the question "can you mentor me?" Mentorships are based on the relationship you have with the other person. Not some purely financial transaction that will be over within 12 months.

Action Guide:

1 - Find a long-term mentor by building relationships with people in your market. A long-term mentor isn't some paid or pro-bono type of relationship. It's more of a father and son one, in a sense that, the mentor passes his knowledge and experience without any type of exchange in money. It's not a formal relationship where the mentor gets paid every month and the mentor and mentee meet 2 hours every month. It's more about the relationship than anything else.

2 - Make the mentoring worth his time by actually taking action and moving towards your goals every day.

3 - Do not put your mentor on a pedestal. Like you, they are imperfect. There will be things about them that will put you off. Just because someone is a good business mentor doesn't mean he's going to be a good example for your family. He may be divorced and alcoholic. He may be someone who has a temper problem. The point is not to copy everything they do. Copy what he's good at and use his "negative traits" as an example of what not to do.

4 - Respect your mentor. He's been through a lot of things more than you do. Remember that he might not be perfect but you chose each other, and you should respect each other's strength and weaknesses.

87 - Be Open to Being Wrong

The most confident people I know are also the humblest ones. They understand that not everything they do will be a success. They know that they can still make mistakes no matter how prepared they are. They know that they can never be perfect - they can only strive for progress.

Some people believe in something so much that they' won't consider the truth anymore. All that matters to them is that they are right - and nothing you could say or do will change their minds. These are people who will never be successful. These are people who already closed their mind on the possibility of being wrong. For them, being right is all that matters. Anything that doesn't support their belief is either wrong or stupid.

Action Guide:

1 - Be open to the idea that you could be wrong.

2 - Consider the facts over your feelings. If all the facts suggest that you are wrong, then you need to admit defeat.

3 - Be open to other people's suggestions.

4 - Be open to having an open conversation with people who disagree with you.

88 - Results in Advance

Learning the process of how you will achieve your goal will boost your confidence because you'll know the exact steps that you need to take to become successful.

The strategy I use is called Results in Advance. It's a reverse engineering process that allows you to know what you need to do to achieve a specific task.

Let's say that you want to make $50,000 this year through Shopify e-commerce.

What you have to do is to breakdown the process into 5-10 steps. These are the things that you need to do to get to $50,000 this year.

For Shopify, you may come up with the following process:

Step 1 - Product Research
Step 2 - Product Sourcing
Step 3 - Website Creation
Step 4 - Running Test Ads
Step 5 - Product Shipping
Step 6 - Running Mass Advertisements

So to achieve your goal, you need to do these 6 things. To increase your chance of hitting your goal, you can also create a sub-category under each step.

In Step 1 - Product Research, you could put the things that you need to do for product research.

Example:

Step 1 - Product Research

- Go to Alibaba and research products
- Search for different categories
- Look at the product reviews

The more detailed your sub-category is, the more likely you are to take action and achieve your goal.

By doing the Results in Advance strategy, you are setting yourself up for a higher probability of success.

Action Guide:

Start reverse engineering your goals. How can you apply the Results in Advance (RIA) strategy in everything you do? Start small if you must. Focus on an easier goal at first and then use RIA strategy as you go for bigger things.

89 - Ask

Want to learn more?

Just ask. Be curious and learn to ask questions.

People who ask questions are people who discover new things. People who go beyond their limits. People who know that the quality of their questions also dictates the quality of their life.

Asking about something you don't understand is a sign of humility. That shows that you're willing to learn and you acknowledge the fact that you don't know about everything. True confidence comes from knowing that you still have a lot to improve on - and that's perfectly fine, because it only means that you still have a lot of room to chase greatness.

Action Guide:

Don't be afraid to look dumb. Ask questions about anything you don't understand.

Look at your field, is there something that you want to know how to do? Is there an idea that you don't understand quite clearly? Ask other people about it, and do it today!

90 - Optimize Your Knowledge for Action

Optimized learning means maximizing your time and your information retention rate. We forget more than half of what we read, study and watch. The faster we use the information and turn it into a specific action, the more we will learn.

So the key is to have a system that optimizes learning. The key is to have a system based on the speed of implementation.

This book is an example of "Speed of Implementation" system. The reason why there's an action guide for each idea in this book is because I want you to optimize your learning for action. I want you to get results. The last thing I want you to do is to read the book and then do nothing. By using the action steps in this book, you'll be able to achieve more things and have lasting change.

You need to do the same when it comes to what you read or study. You need to create an action guide that you can implement as soon as possible. Creating this action guide will force you to solve a problem or do something about the issues you are facing.

Action Guide:

Optimize your knowledge by creating an action guide for every important idea that you learn. Ask yourself, "What is one concrete thing I can do to go from idea to implementation?"

The secret is not in the information itself but rather in the art and speed of execution.

Conclusion

I believe that there are 2 ways to achieve maximum confidence.

The first one is to get it from your family, friends or other people. That means other people's opinion, other people's approval and other people's praise.

The problem with that is you have no control over it.

The second one is to get it from within. That is self-confidence. The type of confidence that you generate for yourself. This is something you can control. It's something that you can have instantly. It's free. It doesn't cost you a penny, and it's something you can generate anytime you want.

The majority of the lessons in this book are based on the second option. I hope that you'll use the practical lessons and I hope that you'll be a more confident version of yourself a few weeks or months from now.

Implement what you identify with and ignore the rest if you want to. My only wish is that you'll give the ideas in this book a try. See what works and see what doesn't. Don't judge the idea by how simple (and how "common sense") it sounds. Remember, common sense doesn't always mean common practice.

Good luck and I wish you all the best in your journey to self-improvement.

-A.V. Mendez

I Need Your Help

If you enjoyed reading this action-packed, daily guide, I would like to request you to leave a short book review on Amazon.

I understand that reviewing a book takes some of your time and I want you to know that I really appreciate you as a reader.

I treat each review as precious and I would really appreciate you taking the time of your day to leave one on the book's Amazon page.

Thanks for reading this book and I will see you on the next one.

OTHER BOOKS BY THE AUTHOR:

Check out the Author's Amazon Page Here:

https://www.amazon.com/AV-Mendez/e/B00XU2UW5S

Milton Keynes UK
Ingram Content Group UK Ltd.
UKHW010702140324
439439UK00016B/1983